more *all-time* favourites *for* ukulele

Wise Publications
part of The Music Sales Group
Copenhagen / Berlin / Madrid / Tokyo

20 075 4185

Published by:
Wise Publications,
14-15 Berners Street, London W1T 3LJ, UK.

Exclusive Distributors:
Music Sales Limited,
Distribution Centre, Newmarket Road, Bury St Edmunds,
Suffolk IP33 3YB, UK.
Music Sales Pty Limited,
20 Resolution Drive, Caringbah, NSW 2229, Australia.

Order No. AM998360
ISBN 978-1-84938-201-4
This book © Copyright 2009 Wise Publications,
a division of Music Sales Limited.

Music arranged and engraved by Shedwork.com
Edited by Tom Farncombe.
Cover designed by Fresh Lemon.
Photographs courtesy of Olivia McGilchrist.

Printed in the EU.

Your Guarantee of Quality
As publishers, we strive to produce every book to the highest
commercial standards.

The music has been freshly engraved and the book has been carefully designed
to minimise awkward page turns and to make playing from it a real pleasure.

Particular care has been given to specifying acid-free, neutral-sized
paper made from pulps which have not been elemental chlorine bleached.

This pulp is from farmed sustainable forests and was produced with
special regard for the environment.

Throughout, the printing and binding have been planned to ensure
a sturdy, attractive publication which should give years of enjoyment.

If your copy fails to meet our high standards, please inform us
and we will gladly replace it.

www.musicsales.com

all things bright and beautiful

Tradition

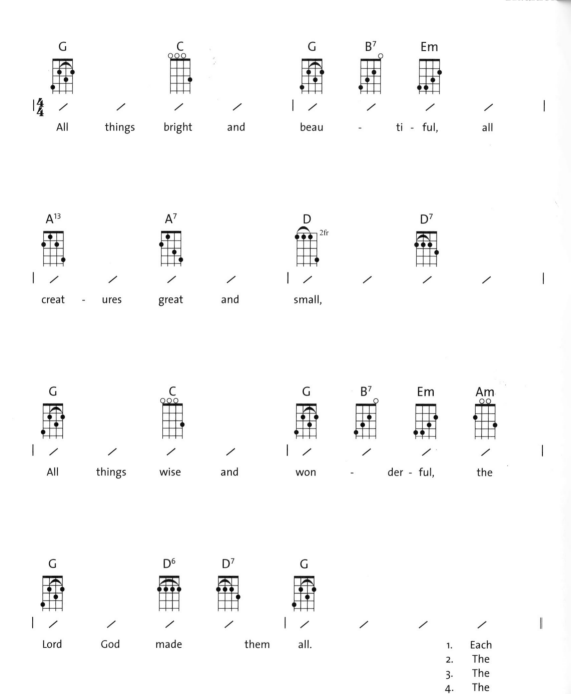

G	C		G	B⁷	Em	
All	things	bright	and	beau	- ti - ful,	all

A¹³	A⁷		D	D⁷	
creat -	ures	great	and	small,	

G	C		G	B⁷	Em	Am
All	things	wise	and	won	- der - ful,	the

G	D⁶	D⁷	G	
Lord	God	made	them	all.

1. Each
2. The
3. The
4. The
5. He

all through the night

Tradition

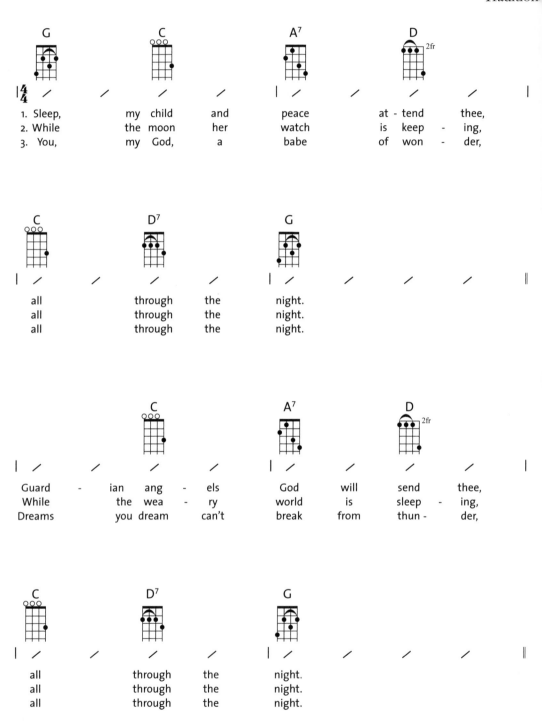

	G	C	A⁷	D
1. Sleep,	my child	and	peace	at - tend thee,
2. While	the moon	her	watch	is keep - ing,
3. You,	my God,	a	babe	of won - der,

	C	D⁷	G
all	through	the	night.
all	through	the	night.
all	through	the	night.

	C	A⁷	D
Guard - ian	ang - els	God	will	send thee,
While	the wea - ry	world	is	sleep - ing,
Dreams	you dream	can't	break	from thun - der,

	C	D⁷	G
all	through	the	night.
all	through	the	night.
all	through	the	night.

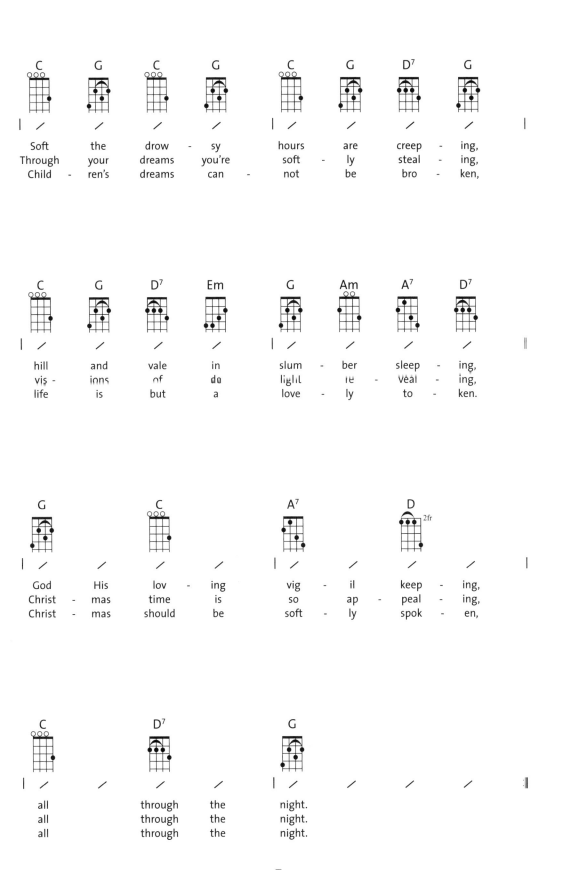

C	G	C	G	C	G	D⁷	G

Soft the drow - sy hours are creep - ing,
Through your dreams you're soft - ly steal - ing,
Child - ren's dreams can - not be bro - ken,

C	G	D⁷	Em	G	Am	A⁷	D⁷

hill and vale in slum - ber sleep - ing,
vis - ions of da light re - veal - ing,
life is but a love - ly to - ken.

G	C	A⁷	D

God His lov - ing vig - il keep - ing,
Christ - mas time is so ap - peal - ing,
Christ - mas should be soft - ly spok - en,

C	D⁷	G

all through the night.
all through the night.
all through the night.

abide with me

Words by Henry Lyte
Music by W.H. Monk

Slow hymn

D · A⁶ · A⁷ · Bm · D⁷ · G · A⁷ · Bm · A⁷

A - bide with me; fast falls the ev - en

D · G · D · G · D

tide; The dark - ness deep - ens;

Em · A · D · E⁷ · A · A⁷ · D · A⁶ · A⁷

Lord with me a - bide; When oth - er

Bm · D⁷ · G · B⁷ · Em

help - ers fail and com - forts flee,

A⁷ · D · A⁷ · D · A⁷ · Bm · G · D · A⁷ · D

Help of the help - less, oh a - bide with me.

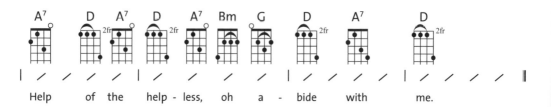

auld lang syne

Traditional

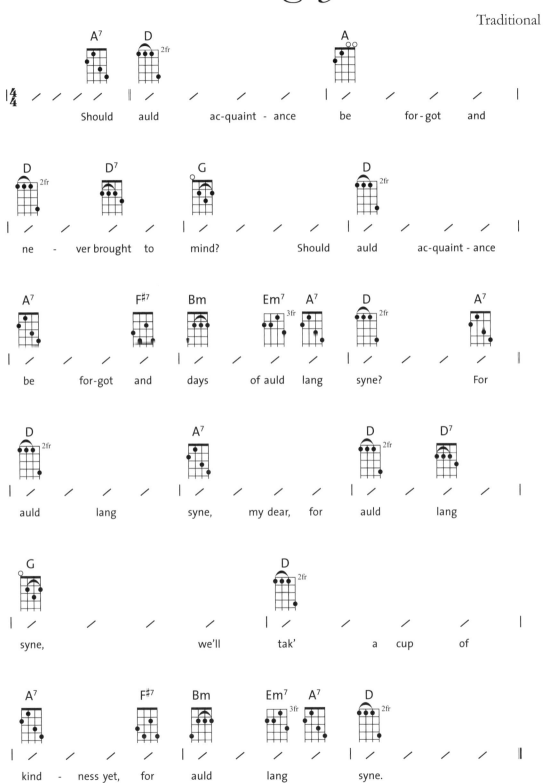

ave maria

Music by Charles Gounod & J.S. Bac

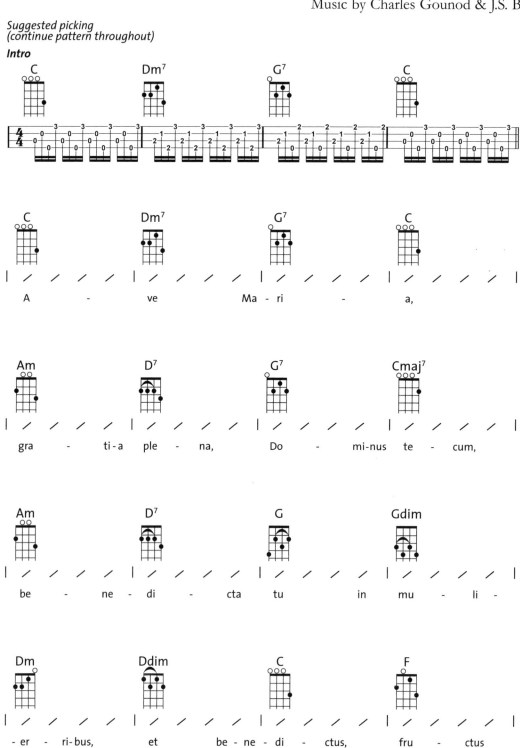

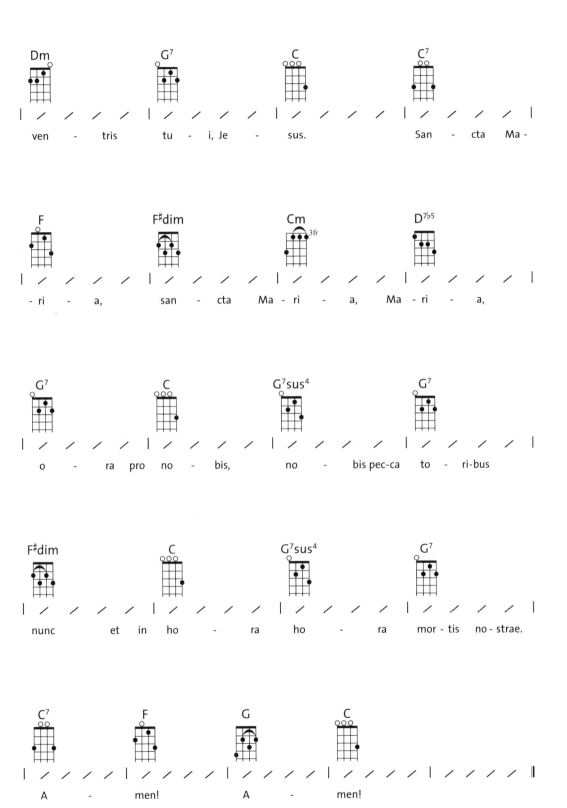

banks of the ohio

Tradition

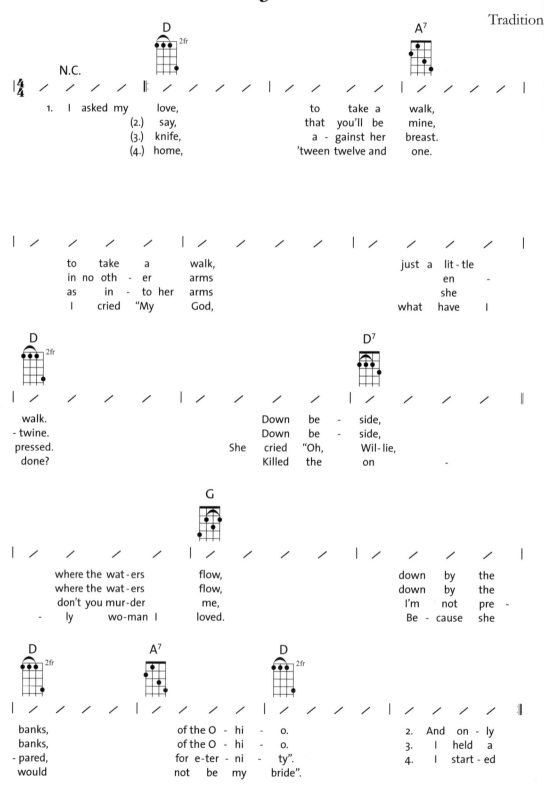

beautiful dreamer

Words & Music by Stephen Foster

1. Beau - ti-ful dream - er, wake un-to me; star - light and dew-drops are wait-ing for thee.
2. Beau - ti-ful dream - er, out in the sea mer-maids are chaunt-ing the wild lo - re - lei.

Sounds of the rude world, heard in the day,
Ov - er the stream - let, vap-ors are borne,

lulled by the moon-light have all passed a - way. Beau-ti-ful dream - er,
wait-ing to fade at the bright com-ing morn. Beau-ti-ful dream - er,

queen of my song, list while I woo thee with soft mel-o - dy.
beam on my heart, e'en on the morn on the steam-let and sea;

Gone are the cares of life's bus - y throng. Beau-ti-ful dream-er, a-wake un-to
Then will all clouds of sor-row de - part. Beau-ti-ful dream-er, a-wake un-to

me! Beau-ti-ful dream-er, a-wake un-to me.
me! Beau-ti-ful dream-er, a-wake un-to me.

a bicycle made for two (daisy bell)

Words & Music by Harry Dacre

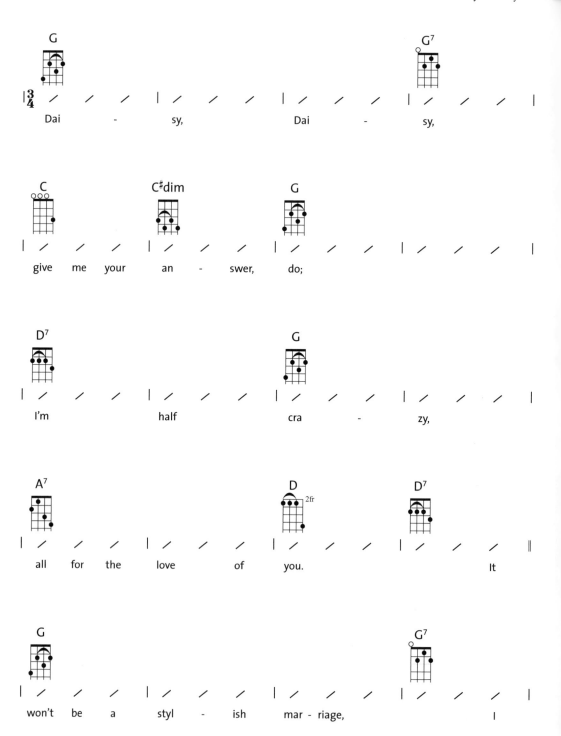

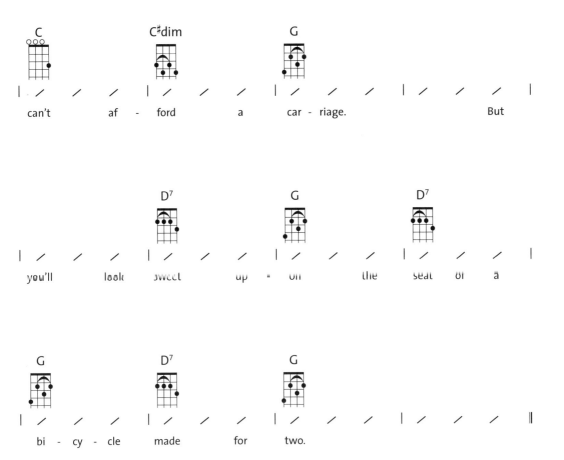

C   C♯dim   G

can't   af - ford   a   car - riage.   But

D⁷   G   D⁷

you'll   look   sweet   up - on   the   seat of a

G   D⁷   G

bi - cy - cle made   for   two.

Verse 2
Henry, Henry, this is my answer true:
I'm not crazy over the likes of you.
If you can't afford a carriage,
Forget about the marriage,
I won't be jammed,
I won't be crammed,
on a bicycle built for two.

bill bailey won't you please come hom

Words & Music by Hughie Canno

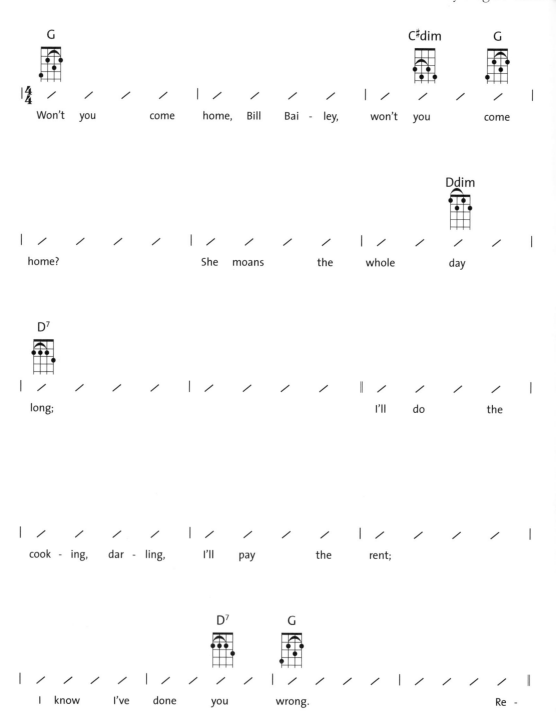

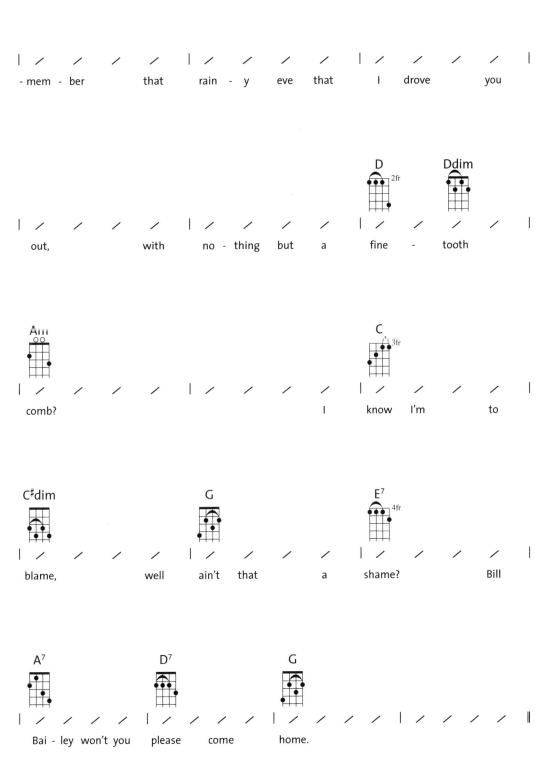

| / / / / | / / / / | / / / / |
- mem - ber that rain - y eve that I drove you

D **Ddim**

| / / / / | / / / / | / / / / |
out, with no - thing but a fine - tooth

Am **C**

| / / / / | / / / / | / / / / |
comb? I know I'm to

C♯dim **G** **E⁷**

| / / / / | / / / / | / / / / |
blame, well ain't that a shame? Bill

A⁷ **D⁷** **G**

| / / / / | / / / / | / / / / | / / / / |
Bai - ley won't you please come home.

17

bingo

Traditional

[Miss out a letter of the word Bingo on each new singing of the verse, replacing it with a clap, sound effect or other fun replacement]

G   C   G   D⁷   G

$\frac{2}{4}$ ╱   ╱ ‖: ╱   ╱ | ╱   ╱ | ╱   ╱ | ╱   ╱ |

There   was a farm-er   had a dog and   Bin-go was his   name - o.

C   D⁷   G

| ╱   ╱ | ╱   ╱ | ╱   ╱ | ╱   ╱ |

B - I - N - G - O,   B - I - N - G - O,
(B) - (I) - N - G - O,   (B) - (I) - N - G - O,
(B) - (I) - (N) - (G) - O,   (B) - (I) - (N) - (G) - O,

Em   Am   D⁷   G

| ╱   ╱ | ╱   ╱ | ╱   ╱ | ╱   ╱ |

B - I - N - G - O,
(B) - (I) - N - G - O, } and   Bin - go was his   name - o. There
(B) - (I) - (N) - (G) - O,

G   C   G   D⁷   G

| ╱   ╱ | ╱   ╱ | ╱   ╱ | ╱   ╱ |

was a farm - er   had a dog and   Bin - go was his   name - o.

C   D⁷   G

| ╱   ╱ | ╱   ╱ | ╱   ╱ | ╱   ╱ |

(B) - I - N - G - O,   (B) - I - N - G - O,
(B) - (I) - (N) - G - O,   (B) - (I) - (N) - G - O,
(B) - (I) - (N) - (G) - (O),   (B) - (I) - (N) - (G) - (O),

Em   Am   D⁷   G

Fine

| ╱   ╱ | ╱   ╱ | ╱   ╱ | ╱   ╱ ‖

(B) - I - N - G - O,
(B) - (I) - (N) - G - O, } and   Bin - go was his   name - o. There
(B) - (I) - (N) - (G) - (O),

clementine

Traditional

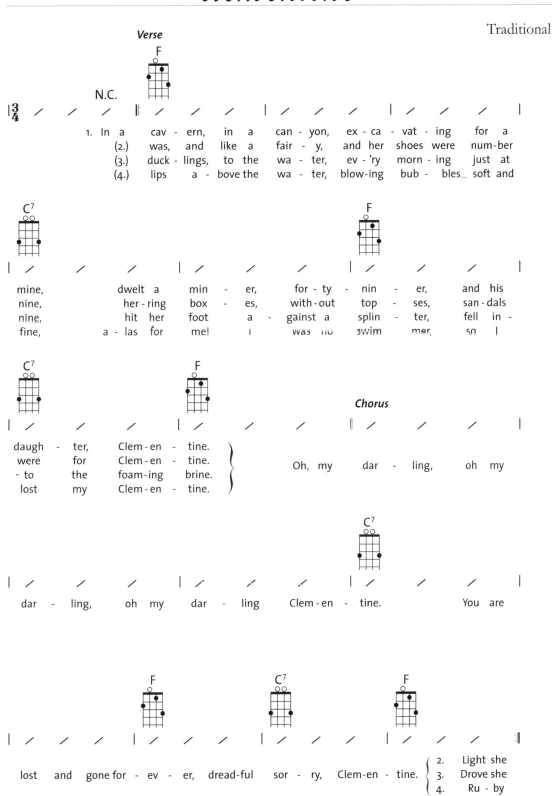

Verse

N.C. | F

3/4

1. In a cav - ern, in a can - yon, ex - ca - vat - ing for a
(2.) was, and like a fair - y, and her shoes were num - ber
(3.) duck - lings, to the wa - ter, ev - 'ry morn - ing just at
(4.) lips a - bove the wa - ter, blow-ing bub - bles_ soft and

C7 | F

mine, dwelt a min - er, for - ty - nin - er, and his
nine, her - ring box - es, with - out top - ses, san - dals
nine, hit her foot a - gainst a splin - ter, fell in -
fine, a - las for me! I was no swim - mer, so I

C7 | F

Chorus

daugh - ter, Clem - en - tine.
were for Clem - en - tine.
- to the foam-ing brine.
lost my Clem - en - tine.

Oh, my dar - ling, oh my

C7

dar - ling, oh my dar - ling Clem - en - tine. You are

F | C7 | F

lost and gone for - ev - er, dread-ful sor - ry, Clem-en - tine.

2. Light she
3. Drove she
4. Ru - by

frog went a-courting

Traditional

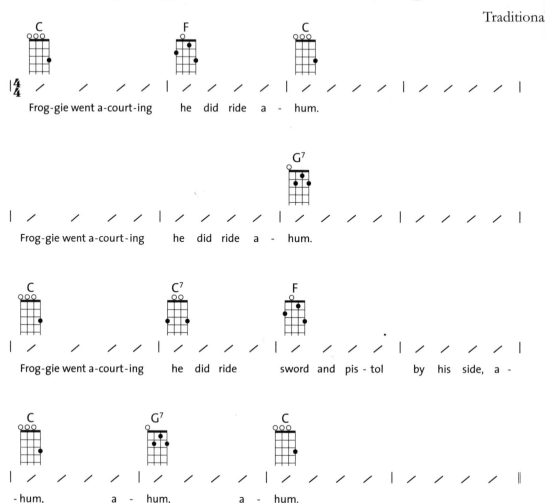

Frog-gie went a-court-ing   he did ride a - hum.

Frog-gie went a-court-ing   he did ride a - hum.

Frog-gie went a-court-ing   he did ride   sword and pis-tol   by his side, a -

- hum,   a - hum,   a - hum.

He rode right up to Miss Mousie's door, ahum
He rode right up to Miss Mousie's door, ahum
He rode right up to Miss Mousie's door
Where he had been many times before, ahum, ahum, ahum.

Said to Miss Mouse, "are you within", ahum
Said to Miss Mouse, "are you within", ahum
Said to Miss Mouse, "are you within"
"Yes, kind sir, I sit and spin", ahum, ahum, ahum.

Took Miss Mousie on his knee, ahum
Took Miss Mousie on his knee, ahum
Took Miss Mousie on his knee
Said, "Miss Mouse, will you marry me?", ahum, ahum, ahum.

Without my Uncle Rat's consent, ahum
Without my Uncle Rat's consent, ahum
Without my Uncle Rat's consent,
I wouldn't marry the president, ahum, ahum, ahum.

Uncle Rat laughed and shook his fat sides, ahum
Uncle Rat laughed and shook his fat sides, ahum
Uncle Rat laughed and shook his fat sides,
To think his niece would be a bride, ahum, ahum, ahum.

Uncle Rat rode into town, ahum
Uncle Rat rode into town, ahum
Uncle Rat rode into town,
To buy his niece a wedding gown, ahum, ahum, ahum.

Where will the wedding supper be, ahum
Where will the wedding supper be, ahum,
Where will the wedding supper be,
Way down yonder in a hollow tree, ahum, ahum, ahum.

What will the wedding supper be, ahum
What will the wedding supper be, ahum
What will the wedding supper be,
A fried mosquito and a black-eyed bee, ahum, ahum, ahum.

The first guest in was a bumble-bee, ahum
The first guest in was a bumble-bee, ahum
The first guest in was a bumble-bee,
He danced a jig with a crooked back flea, ahum, ahum, ahum.

The next guest in was a little black tic, ahum
The next guest in was a little black tic, ahum
The next guest in was a little black tic,
And he ate so much he made himself sick, ahum, ahum, ahum.

They all went sailing across the lake, ahum
They all went sailing across the lake, ahum
They all went sailing across the lake,
And they got swallowed up by a big black snake, ahum, ahum, ahum.

There's bread and cheese upon the shelf, ahum
There's bread and cheese upon the shelf, ahum
There's bread and cheese upon the shelf,
If you want any more, you can sing it yourself, ahum, ahum, ahum.

it's a long way to tipperary

Words & Music by Jack Judge & Harry Williams

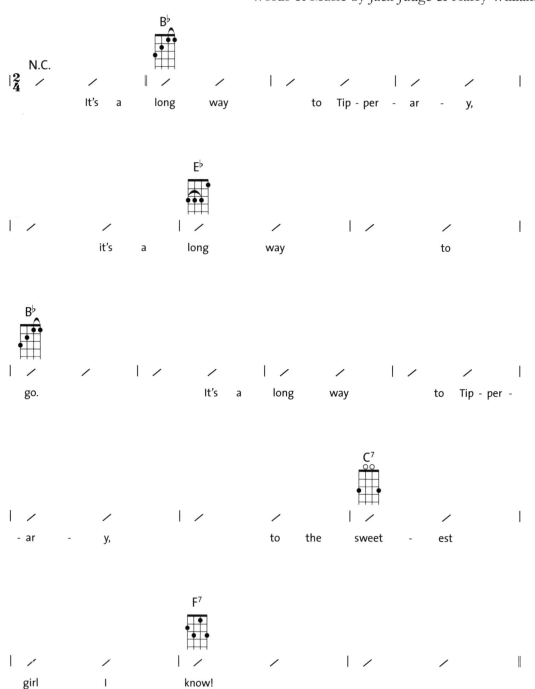

It's a long way to Tip - per - ar - y,

it's a long way to

go. It's a long way to Tip - per -

- ar - y, to the sweet - est

girl I know!

keep on the sunny side

Words by Ada Blenkhorn
Music by J. Howard Entwhistle

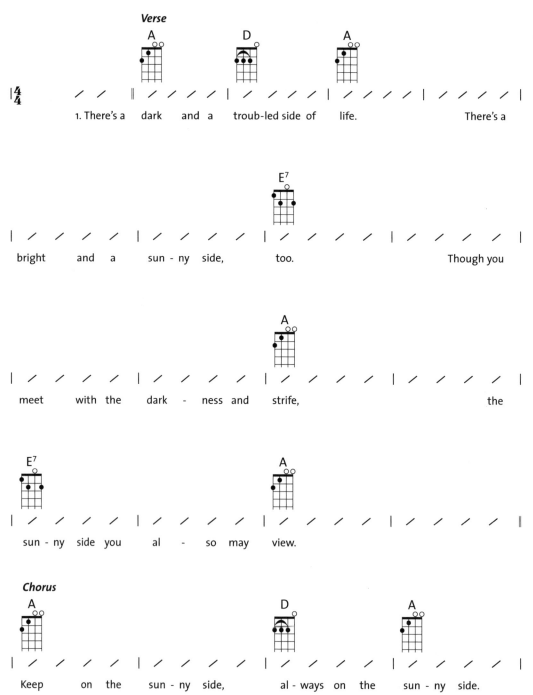

Verse

1. There's a dark and a troub-led side of life. There's a bright and a sun - ny side, too. Though you meet with the dark - ness and strife, the sun - ny side you al - so may view.

Chorus

Keep on the sun - ny side, al - ways on the sun - ny side.

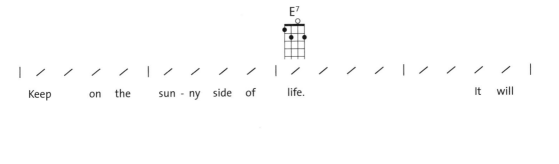

Keep   on the sun - ny side of   life.   It will

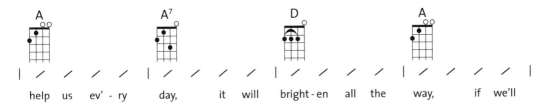

help us ev' - ry   day,   it will bright - en all the   way,   if we'll

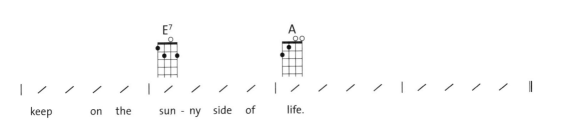

keep   on the sun - ny side of   life.

Verse 2
Oh the storm and its fury broke today
Crushing hopes that we cherish so dear
The clouds and storm will in time pass away
The sun again will shine bright and clear.

Verse 3
Let us greet with a song of hope each day
Though the moment be cloudy or fair
Let us trust in our Saviour always
To keep us every one in His care.

la cucaracha

Traditional

Verse

G

Cuan - do un - o quiere a un - a,
When a fel - low loves a maid - en,

D⁷

y es - ta un - a no lo quiere.
and that maid - en does - n't love him,

Es lo mis - mo que si un cal - vo,
It's the same as when a bald man,

G

en la cal - le en - cuentr' un peine. La cu - ca -
finds a comb up - on the high - way. The cu - ca -

Chorus

D⁷

- ra - cha, la cu-ca - ra - cha, Ya no quier - es cam - in - ar, por - que no
- ra - cha, the cu-ca - ra - cha, Does - n't want to car - ry on, be - cause she

| ⁄ | ⁄ | ⁄ | ⁄ | | ⁄ | ⁄ | ⁄ | ⁄ | |

tien - es,   por - que   no   fal - ta.
has - n't,   oh   no   she   has - n't,

G

| ⁄ | ⁄ | ⁄ | ⁄ | | ⁄ | ⁄ | ⁄ | ⁄ | |

ma - ri - hua - na   que   fu - mar.
ma - ri - hua - na   for   to   smoke.

Verse 2
Las muchachas son de oro;
Las casadas son de plata;
Las viudas son de cobre,
Y las viejas oja de lata.

Verse 2
All the maidens are of pure gold;
All the married girls are silver;
All the widows are of copper,
And old women merely tin.

Verse 3
Mi vecina de enfrente
Se llamaba Doña Clara,
Y si no había muerto
Es probable se llamara.

Verse 3
My neighbour across the highway
Used to be called Doña Clara,
And if she has not expired
Likely that's her name tomorrow.

Verse 4
Las muchachas de Las Vegas
Son muy altas y delgaditas,
Pero son mas pedigueñas
Que las animas benditas.

Verse 4
All the girls up at Las Vegas
Are most awful tall and skinny,
But they're worse for plaintive pleading
Than the souls in Purgatory.

Verse 5
Las muchachas de la villa
No saben ni dar un beso,
Cuando las de Albuquerque
Hasta estiran el pescuezo.

Verse 5
All the girls here in the city
Don't know how to give you kisses,
While the ones from Albuquerque
Stretch their necks to avoid misses.

Verse 6
Las muchachas Mexicanas
Son lindas como una flor,
Y hablan tan dulcemente
Que encantan de amor.

Verse 6
All the girls from Mexico
Are as pretty as a flower,
And they talk so very sweetly
Fill your heart quite up with love.

london bridge

Tradition

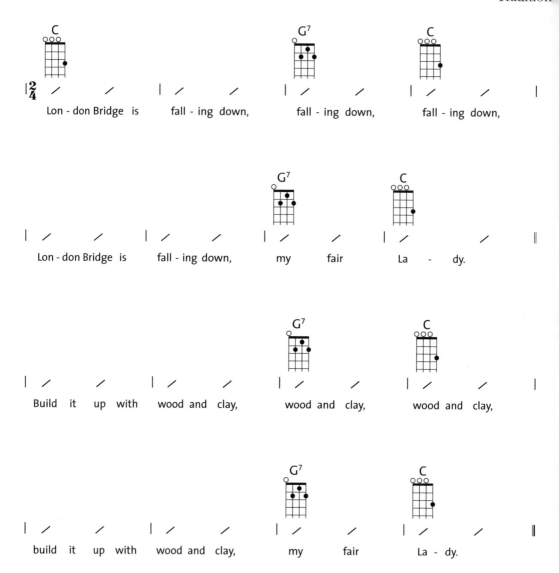

Lon - don Bridge is fall - ing down, fall - ing down, fall - ing down,

Lon - don Bridge is fall - ing down, my fair La - dy.

Build it up with wood and clay, wood and clay, wood and clay,

build it up with wood and clay, my fair La - dy.

Wood and clay will wash away,
Wash away, wash away,
Wood and clay will wash away,
My fair Lady.

Build it up with bricks and mortar,
Bricks and mortar, bricks and mortar,
Build it up with bricks and mortar,
My fair Lady.

Bricks and mortar will not stay,
Will not stay, will not stay,
Bricks and mortar will not stay,
My fair Lady.

Build it up with iron and steel,
Iron and steel, iron and steel,
Build it up with iron and steel,
My fair Lady.

Iron and steel will bend and bow,
Bend and bow, bend and bow,
Iron and steel will bend and bow,
My fair Lady.

Build it up with silver and gold,
Silver and gold, silver and gold,
Build it up with silver and gold,
My fair Lady.

Silver and gold will be stolen away,
Stolen away, stolen away,
Silver and gold will be stolen away,
My fair Lady.

Set a man to watch all night,
Watch all night, watch all night,
Set a man to watch all night,
My fair Lady.

Suppose the man should fall asleep,
Fall asleep, fall asleep,
Suppose the man should fall asleep?
My fair Lady.

Give him a pipe to smoke all night,
Smoke all night, smoke all night,
Give him a pipe to smoke all night,
My fair Lady.

men of harlech

Welsh Traditional Song

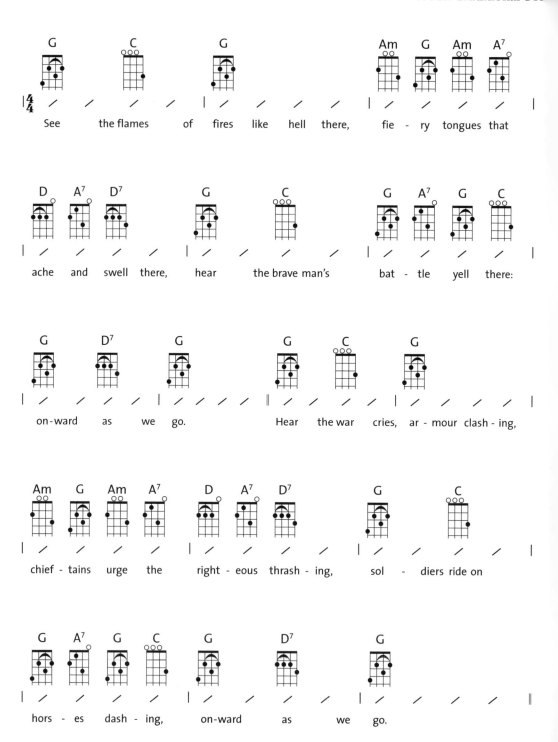

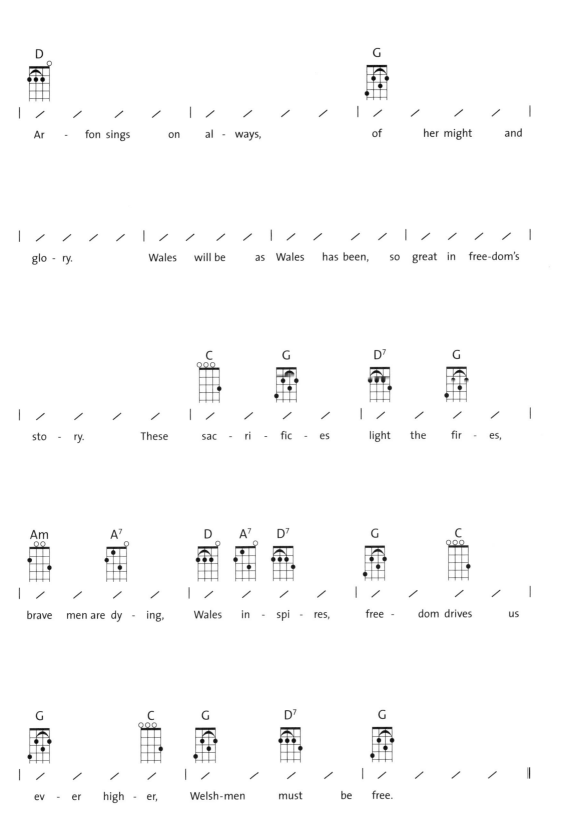

D   G

| /   /   /   / | /   /   /   / | /   /   /   / |

Ar - fon sings on al - ways,   of her might and

| /   /   /   / | /   /   /   / | /   /   /   / | /   /   /   / |

glo - ry.   Wales will be as Wales has been, so great in free-dom's

C   G   D⁷   G

| /   /   /   / | /   /   /   / | /   /   /   / |

sto - ry.   These sac - ri - fic - es light the fir - es,

Am   A⁷   D   A⁷   D⁷   G   C

| /   /   /   / | /   /   /   / | /   /   /   / |

brave men are dy - ing, Wales in - spi - res, free - dom drives us

G   C   G   D⁷   G

| /   /   /   / | /   /   /   / | /   /   /   / ‖

ev - er high - er, Welsh-men must be free.

michael row the boat ashore

Traditional

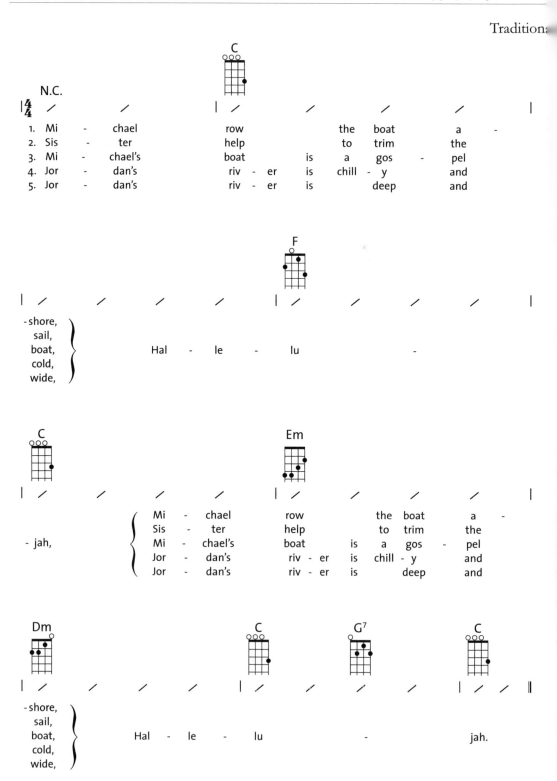

rock-a-bye, baby

Traditional

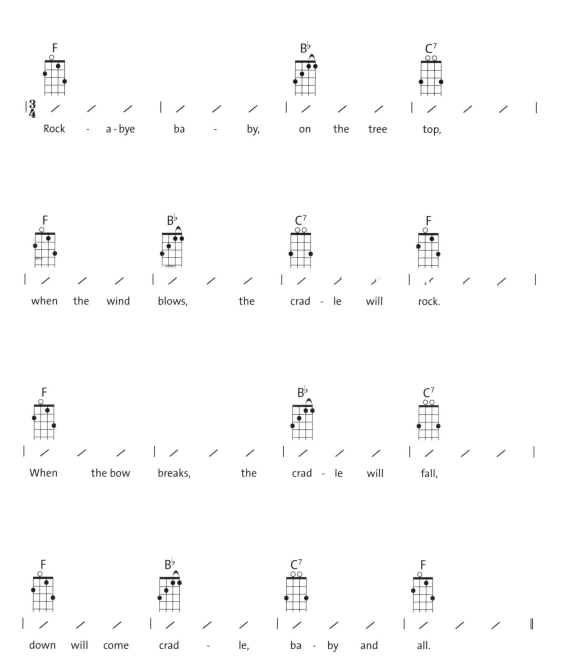

Rock - a-bye ba - by, on the tree top,

when the wind blows, the crad - le will rock.

When the bow breaks, the crad - le will fall,

down will come crad - le, ba - by and all.

she'll be coming 'round the mountair

Tradition:

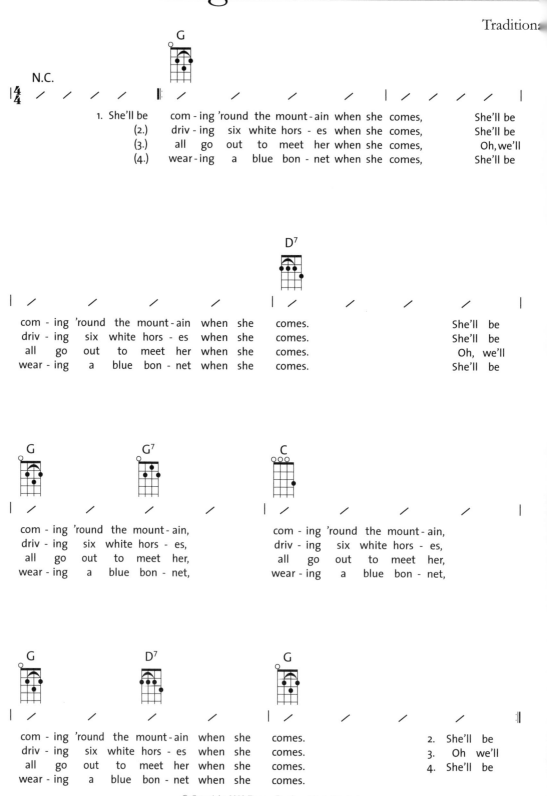

sing a song of sixpence

Traditional

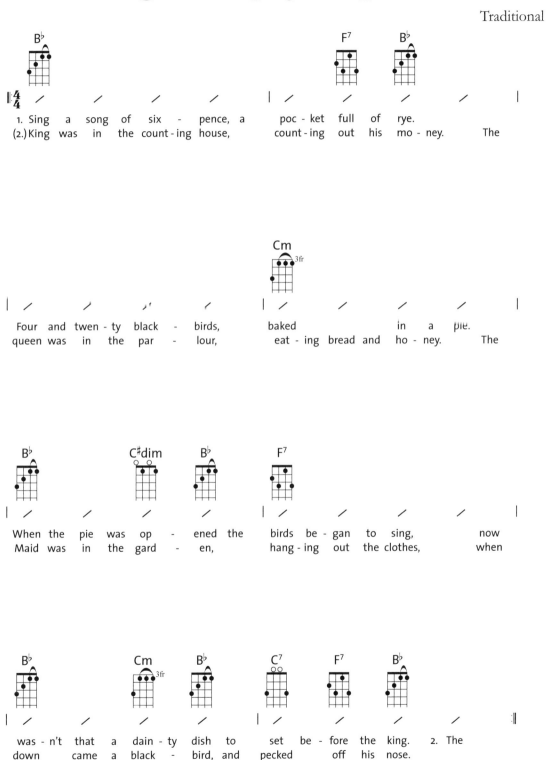

the star spangled banner

Words by Francis Scott Ke
Music by John Stafford Smit

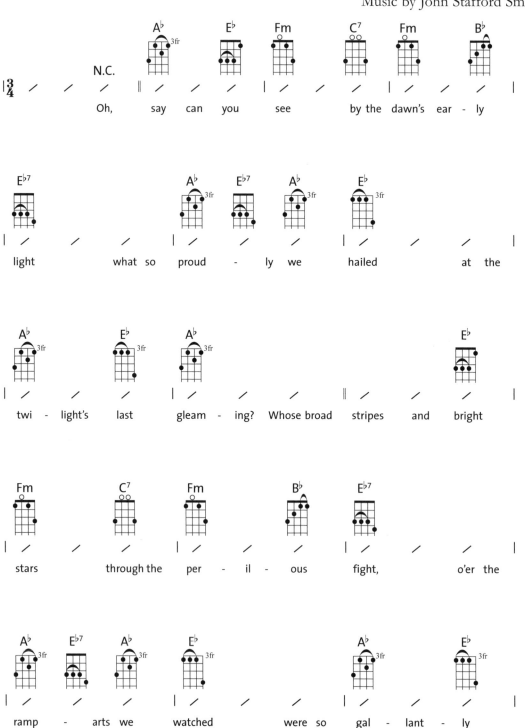

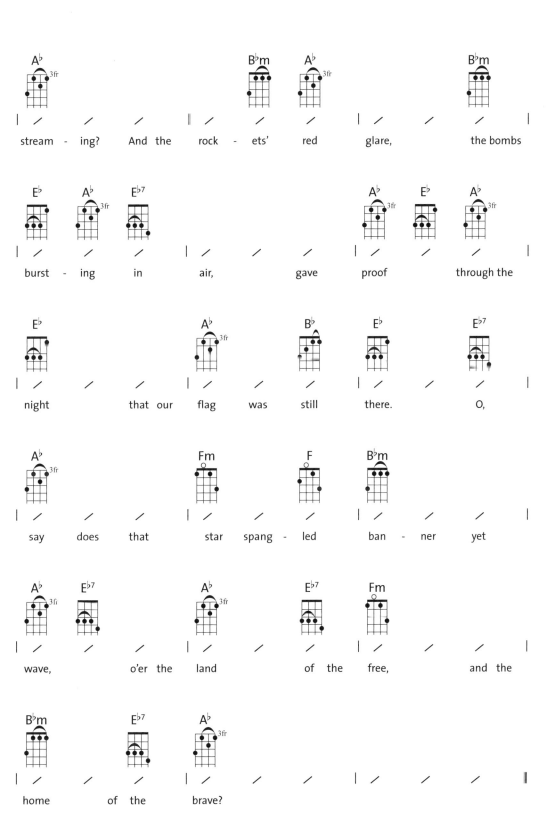

swing low, sweet chariot

Tradition

Chorus

D · Bm · · · | Em · A⁷ · · |

Swing   low,   sweet   char - i - ot,

Bm · · F♯m · · | Em · A⁷ · · |

com - ing for to car - ry me   home.

D · D⁷ · · | G · Em A⁷ · |

Swing   low,   sweet   char - i - ot,

D G Em A⁷ · | D · · · ‖

com - ing for to car - ry me   home.

1. |
2. If

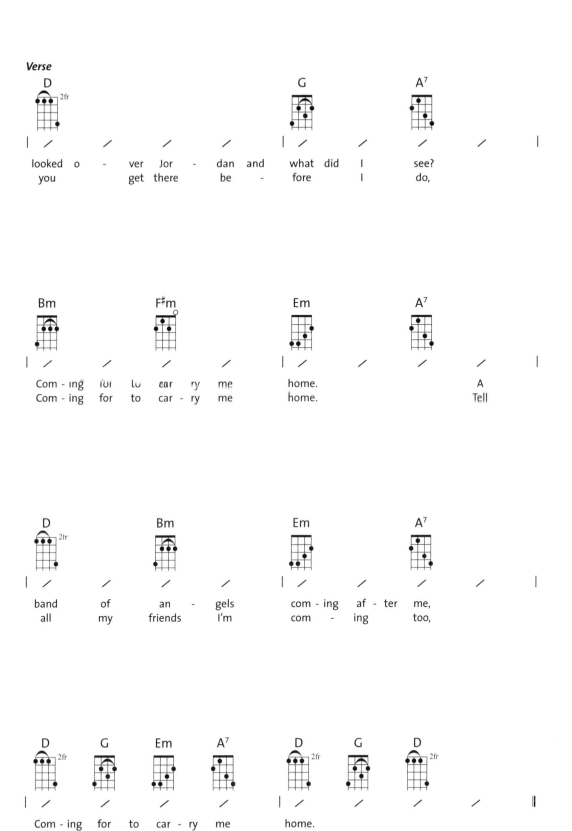

Verse

D   G   A⁷

looked o - ver Jor - dan and what did I see?
you   get there be - fore I do,

Bm   F♯m   Em   A⁷

Com - ing for to car - ry me home.   A
Com - ing for to car - ry me home.   Tell

D   Bm   Em   A⁷

band of an - gels com - ing af - ter me,
all my friends I'm com - ing too,

D G Em A⁷   D G D

Com - ing for to car - ry me home.
Com - ing for to car - ry me home.

39

there is a tavern in the town

Traditional

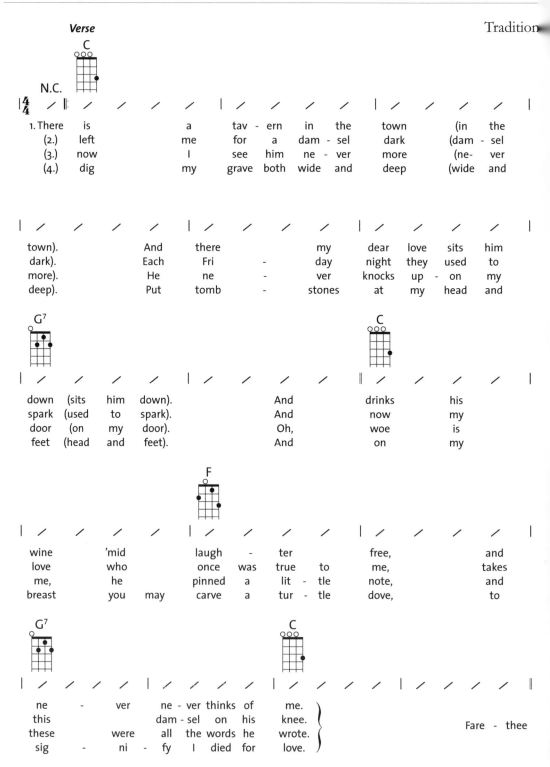

Verse

N.C. / C

1. There is   a   tav - ern   in   the   town   (in   the
(2.) left   me   for   a   dam - sel   dark   (dam - sel
(3.) now   I   see   him   ne - ver   more   (ne - ver
(4.) dig   my   grave   both   wide   and   deep   (wide   and

town).   And   there   my   dear   love   sits   him
dark).   Each   Fri   -   day   night   they   used   to
more).   He   ne   -   ver   knocks   up - on   my
deep).   Put   tomb   -   stones   at   my   head   and

G⁷

down   (sits   him   down).   And   drinks   his
spark (used   to   spark).   And   now   my
door   (on   my   door).   Oh,   woe   is
feet   (head   and   feet).   And   on   my

C

F

wine   'mid   laugh - ter   free,   and
love   who   once   was   true   to   me,   takes
me,   he   pinned   a   lit - tle   note,   and
breast   you   may   carve   a   tur - tle   dove,   to

G⁷   C

ne - ver   ne - ver   thinks   of   me.
this   dam - sel   on   his   knee.
these   were   all   the   words   he   wrote.
sig - ni - fy   I   died   for   love.

Fare - thee

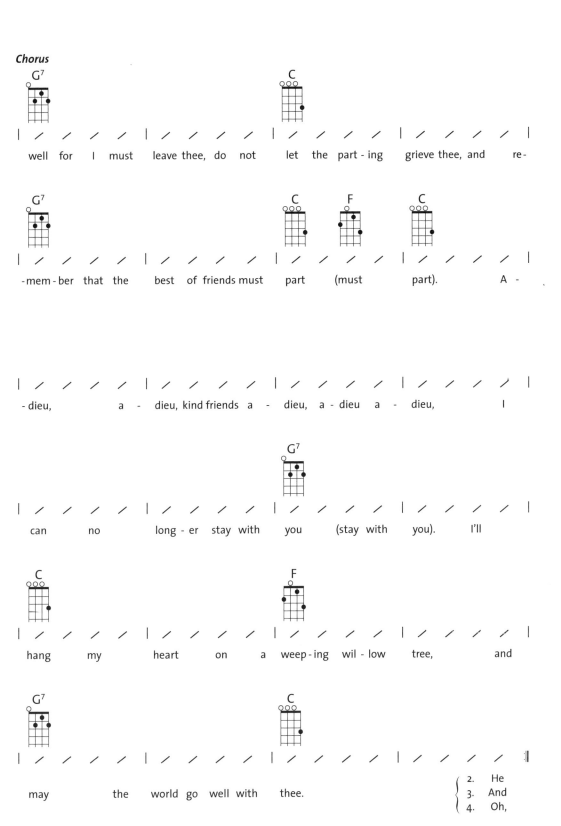

Chorus

G⁷ · · · · | · · · · | C · · · · | · · · · | · · · · |

well   for   I   must   leave thee,   do   not   let   the   part-ing   grieve thee,   and   re-

G⁷ · · · · | · · · · | C · · · · F | C · · · · | · · · · |

-mem-ber   that   the   best   of friends must   part   (must   part).   A -

| · · · · | · · · · | · · · · | · · · · | · · · · |

- dieu,   a   -   dieu, kind friends a   -   dieu,   a - dieu   a - dieu,   I

G⁷ · · · · | · · · · | · · · · | · · · · | · · · · |

can   no   long-er   stay with   you   (stay with   you).   I'll

C · · · · | · · · · | F · · · · | · · · · | · · · · |

hang   my   heart   on   a   weep-ing   wil-low   tree,   and

G⁷ · · · · | · · · · | C · · · · | · · · · | · · · · ‖

may   the   world   go   well with   thee.

⎧ 2.   He
⎨ 3.   And
⎩ 4.   Oh,

this little light of mine

Tradition

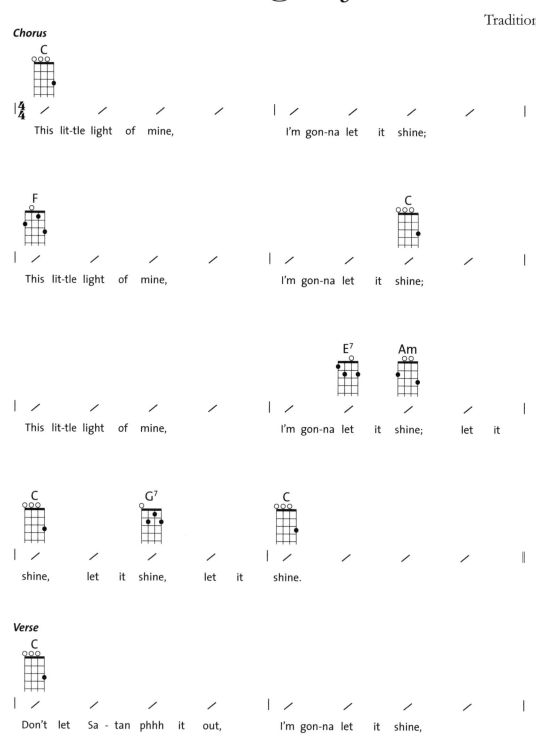

Chorus

C

This lit-tle light of mine,   I'm gon-na let it shine;

F   C

This lit-tle light of mine,   I'm gon-na let it shine;

E⁷   Am

This lit-tle light of mine,   I'm gon-na let it shine;   let it

C   G⁷   C

shine,   let it shine,   let it shine.

Verse

C

Don't let Sa - tan phhh it out,   I'm gon-na let it shine,

F   C

| / | / | / | / | | / | / | / | / | |

Don't let Sa - tan phhh it out,   I'm gon-na let   it   shine,

E^7 Am

| / | / | / | / | | / | / | / | / | |

Don't let Sa - tan phhh it out,   I'm gon-na let   it   shine,   let   it

C G^7 C

| / | / | / | / | | / | / | / | / | ‖

shine,   let   it   shine,   let   it   shine.

Verse 2
Hide it under a bushel, no!
I'm gonna let it shine;
Hide it under a bushel, no!
I'm gonna let it shine;
Hide it under a bushel, no!
I'm gonna let it shine;
Let it shine, let it shine,
let it shine.

Verse 3
Let it shine till Jesus comes,
I'm gonna let it shine;
Let it shine till Jesus comes,
I'm gonna let it shine;
Let it shine till Jesus comes,
I'm gonna let it shine;
Let it shine, let it shine,
let it shine.

we wish you a merry christmas

Tradition

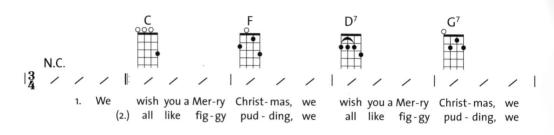

1. We wish you a Mer-ry Christ-mas, we wish you a Mer-ry Christ-mas, we
(2.) all like fig-gy pud-ding, we all like fig-gy pud-ding, we

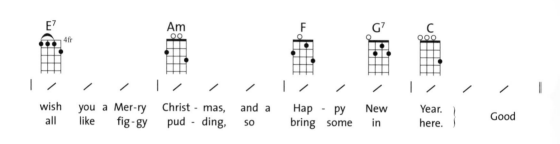

wish you a Mer-ry Christ-mas, and a Hap-py New Year. } Good
all like fig-gy pud-ding, so bring some in here. }

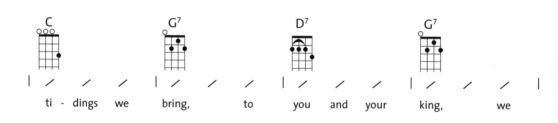

ti-dings we bring, to you and your king, we

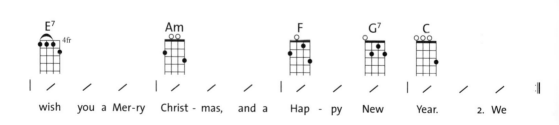

wish you a Mer-ry Christ-mas, and a Hap-py New Year. 2. We

when the saints go marching in

Traditional

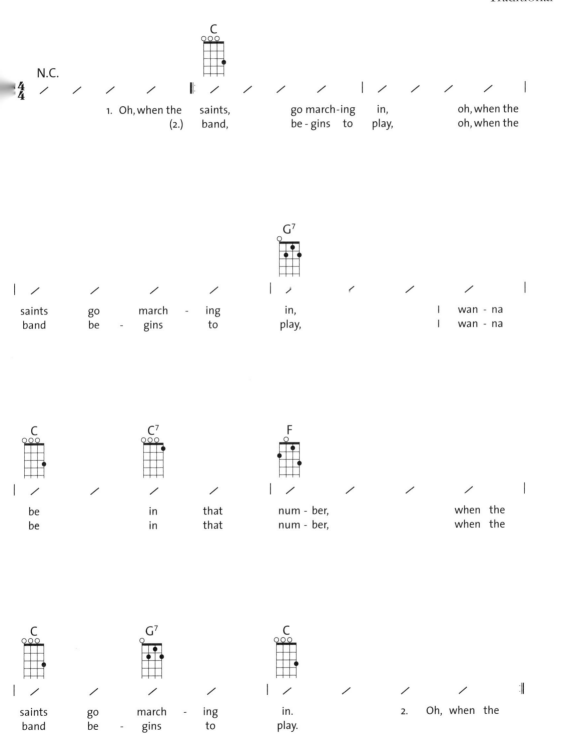

whiskey in the jar

Traditional

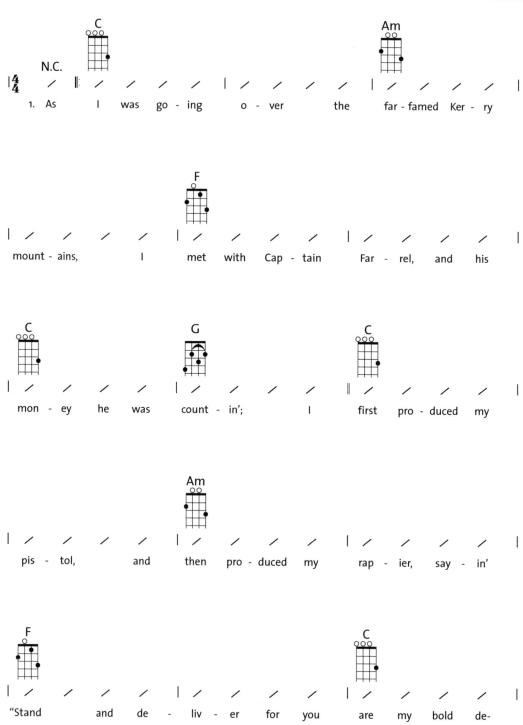

1. As I was go - ing o - ver the far - famed Ker - ry mount - ains, I met with Cap - tain Far - rel, and his mon - ey he was count - in'; I first pro - duced my pis - tol, and then pro - duced my rap - ier, say - in' "Stand and de - liv - er for you are my bold de-

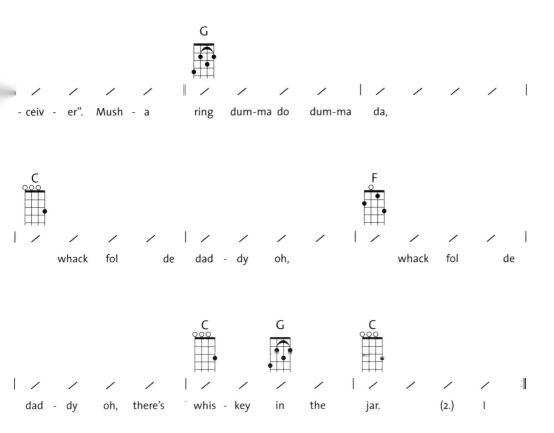

G
- ceiv - er". Mush - a   ring dum-ma do dum-ma da,

C   F
whack   fol   de   dad - dy   oh,   whack   fol   de

C   G   C
dad - dy   oh, there's   whis - key   in   the   jar.   (2.)

Verse 2
I counted out his money and it made a pretty penny,
I put it in my pocket, and I took it home to Jenny,
She sighed, and she swore that she never would deceive me,
But the devil takes the women for they never can be easy.

Verse 3
I went into my chamber all for to take a slumber,
I dreamt of gold and jewels and for sure it was no wonder,
But Jenny drew my charges and she filled them out with water,
Then sent for Captain Farrel, to be ready for the slaughter.

Verse 4
'Twas early in the morning just before I rose to travel,
Up comes a band of footmen and likewise, Captain Farrel,
I first produced my pistol for she stole away my rapier,
But I couldn't shoot the water, so a prisoner I was taken.

Verse 5
If anyone can aid me 'tis my brother in the army,
If I can find his station, in Cork or in Killarney,
And if he'll go with me we'll go roving in Kilkenny,
And I'm sure he'll treat me better than my darling sporting Jenny.

123456789